Smithsonian

# THE GREENSBORO LUNCH COUNTER

## What an Artifact Can Tell Us About the Civil Rights Movement

by Shawn Pryor

CAPSTONE PRESS
a capstone imprint

Capstone Captivate is published by Capstone Press,
an imprint of Capstone.
1710 Roe Crest Drive
North Mankato, Minnesota 56003
www.capstonepub.com

**Library of Congress Cataloging-in-Publication Data is available on the Library
of Congress website.**
ISBN 978-1-4966-9580-2 (hardcover)
ISBN 978-1-4966-9684-7 (paperback)
ISBN 978-1-9771-5503-0 (eBook PDF)

Summary: On February 1, 1960, four young black men sat down at a Woolworth's
lunch counter in Greensboro, North Carolina, and staged a nonviolent protest
against segregation. Soon, thousands of students were staging sit-ins in 55 cities
in 13 states. How did a lunch counter become a symbol of civil rights? Readers
will find out the answer to this question and what an artifact can tell us about
U.S. civil rights history.

**Image Credits**
Associated Press: 14, 22, Atlanta Journal-Constitution, 19, News & Record/
Joseph Rodriguez, 36, News & Record/Lynn Hey, 26, Ruth Fremson, 32; Getty
Images: Bettmann, cover (back), 20, 21, 25 (bottom), Carnegie Museum of Art/
Charles "Teenie" Harris, 13, The LIFE Images Collection/Lynn Pelham, 27,
The Washington Post/Ricky Carioti, 40, 41; Granger: 17; LBJ Library: Photo
by O.J. Rapp, 31; Library of Congress: 5, 8, 10, 28, 30, Photographs in Carol
M. Highsmith's America Project in the Carol M. Highsmith Archive, 15, 45;
Newscom: Everett Collection, 6, 23, 25 (top), Polaris/News & Record/Jerry
Wolford, 43 (top); North Wind Picture Archives: 9; Shutterstock: Andrea Izzotti, 7,
Anthony J. Davis, 39, Peter Hermes Furian, 29, V_E, 44; Smithsonian Institution:
National Museum of American History, 11, National Museum of American
History/Photo by Hugh Talman, cover (bottom right), 1, 12, 35, National
Museum of American History/Photo by Jaclyn Nash, 43 (bottom), National
Museum of American History/Photo by Richard Strauss, 43 (middle)

**Editorial Credits**
Editor: Mandy Robbins; Designer: Tracy Davies; Media Researcher:
Svetlana Zhurkin; Production Specialist: Tori Abraham

All internet sites appearing in back matter were available and accurate when this
book was sent to press.

# TABLE OF CONTENTS

Words in **bold** are in the glossary.

# Chapter 1
# TAKING A STAND

On February 1, 1960, Ezell A. Blair Jr., Franklin E. McCain, David L. Richmond, and Joseph A. McNeil walked into the Woolworth's store in Greensboro, North Carolina. The four young Black men wanted to take a stand against **segregation**.

**Slavery** had ended in the United States almost 100 years earlier, after the Civil War (1861–1865). But the war hadn't ended **racism**. Segregation laws in the South kept Black people separate from whites. They had separate schools and housing. They had separate seating in buses and restaurants. They even had separate public bathrooms and drinking fountains. But separate was not equal. Black people almost always had worse facilities than whites. In many places, Black people were denied service altogether.

The Woolworth's lunch counter in Greensboro was segregated, but the shopping area of the store wasn't. Black people could spend their money at the store. They could even order food from the lunch counter.

A sign marking a segregated bus station waiting room in Durham, North Carolina

What Black people weren't allowed to do was sit at the lunch counter. So how did these four young men take a stand? By taking a seat. In doing this, they turned a simple lunch counter into a historical **artifact**.

## Living in Poverty

Segregation laws made it difficult for Black people to access well-paying jobs. In 1959, Black people made up about 10 percent of the total U.S. population. But they made up 55.1 percent of people living in poverty.

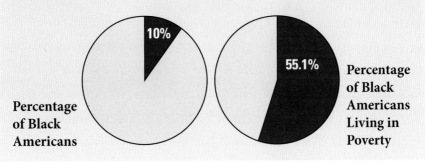

10%

Percentage of Black Americans

55.1%

Percentage of Black Americans Living in Poverty

# Chapter 2
# WHO, WHAT, WHY, AND WHERE?

The brave young men came to be called the Greensboro Four. They were students at North Carolina Agricultural and Technical College (A&T), a historically Black college. They were tired of segregation and being treated as though they were worth less than white people.

A Black teenager named Emmett Till (left) was murdered by white men in Mississippi in 1955.

The Greensboro Four were also moved by the murder of Emmett Till a few years back. Had he lived, Till would have been about their age. In 1955, Till was a 14-year-old Black boy who had been accused of whistling at a white woman in Mississippi. Because of this, two white men beat and murdered him. A court found the men not guilty, but they later confessed. Till's murderers never faced justice.

The Greensboro Four were inspired by the peaceful protests happening around the world. Some were nearby, like the U.S.-based Congress for Racial Equality (CORE). This group trained protesters on how to not respond to verbal or physical attacks. In 1947, CORE organized **activists** who rode in buses across the South to protest segregated bus travel between states. Other peaceful protests had been far away, such as those led by lawyer and activist Mahatma Gandhi. His nonviolent movement in India in the early 1900s ended 200 years of British rule.

Mahatma Gandhi statue

The Civil rights movement had already made major strides before the Greensboro sit-ins. In 1948, President Harry S. Truman ended segregation in the military. In 1954, the Supreme Court ruled segregation **unconstitutional** in public schools. In 1955, Rosa Parks refused to give up her seat in the whites-only section of a segregated bus. This act sparked the bus boycott in Montgomery, Alabama. It led to the **integration** of buses throughout the country. In the late 1950s, Black pastors and civil rights leaders, including Dr. Martin Luther King Jr., continued to use peaceful protests to fight **discrimination** against Black people.

A group of schoolchildren at the recently integrated Barnard school in Washington, D.C., in 1955

While Black people were making progress, the Greensboro Four didn't expect change to come easily. Local governments and businesses in the South still held tightly to racist policies. Previous sit-ins had been unsuccessful. In 1957, a group of protesters tried to end segregation at the Royal Ice Cream Parlor in Durham, North Carolina. They failed.

## Reconstruction: Ground Gained and Lost

After the Civil War, 4 million formerly enslaved people became U.S. citizens with the passage of the 14th Amendment. At first, the government passed laws called "black codes" to restrict the rights of Black people. Most Northerners disagreed with this idea. They voted in new lawmakers who overturned the black codes, giving Black Americans full rights. Between 1867 and 1877,

The 1873 South Carolina legislature had several Black members.

about 2,000 Black people were voted into public office. As a reaction, Southern states soon passed the segregation laws that would hold Black Americans back for almost 100 more years.

So how did Woolworth's fit into this situation? F.W. Woolworth's was a general store chain started in 1879. The stores were popular across the United States from 1912 to the 1980s. Woolworth's was one of the most popular five-and-dime stores. A five-and-dime store was like today's dollar stores. Everything was low in cost, and many things were sold there. The stores served lower middle-class or working-class people.

Shoppers in a Washington, D.C., Woolworth's in the mid-1900s

By the 1960s, most Woolworth's stores had lunch counters. Customers could shop and then stop at the counter for a bite to eat. Black Americans who went to the F.W. Woolworth's in Greensboro, North Carolina, could shop in the store. They also

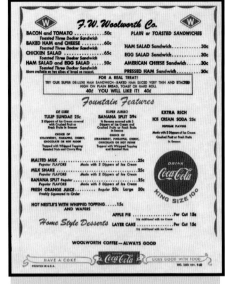

A Woolworth's lunch counter menu

worked at the lunch counter as waitstaff and kitchen staff. But because of segregation, Black people could not sit at the lunch counter. If they ordered food, they had to do so at a "stand-up counter" and take their food to go. To Black people, the **vinyl**, metal-backed seats stretching the length of the lunch counter, were a symbol of the discrimination they faced every day.

## FACT!

In 1979, Woolworth's was the largest department store chain in the world. But by 1997, all U.S. Woolworth's stores were out of business, due to competition from other retailers such as Walmart and Target.

## Chapter 3
# TAKING ACTION

Today, a piece of the Greensboro lunch counter and four stools sit at the Smithsonian's National Museum of American History in Washington, D.C. Another piece remains in the International Civil Rights Center & Museum, located at the site of the former Greensboro Woolworth's store. But on February 1, 1960, the stools and lunch counter still sat in the Greensboro store. And that is where Blair, McCain, Richmond, and McNeil were heading. But first, they stopped at Ralph Johns's store.

A portion of the Greensboro Woolworth's lunch counter on display at the National Museum of American History

An NAACP event in Pennsylvania in 1959

Johns was a local businessman and a white Syrian immigrant. He was also the first non-Black member of the Greensboro chapter of the National Association for the Advancement of Colored People (NAACP). Johns had suggested protesting segregated restaurants to the NAACP for more than 10 years. He wanted to help because he understood that segregation was wrong and unjust.

**FACT!**

Johns would often put signs in his store's window with slogans such as, "God Hates Segregation."

The Greensboro Four had been discussing staging a sit-in at the Woolworth's lunch counter for weeks, if not months. They stopped by Johns's store to tell him they were going to take his suggestion. Johns gave the men money to buy small items at the store before they sat down at the lunch counter. He told them to have their receipts out to prove that they were paying customers.

In the meantime, Johns planned to contact the local media to cover the story. He fully expected the police to be called, and he wanted local reporters there as witnesses. They would see that the four young men weren't causing trouble. They could show the racism that the young men faced and help get community support.

Franklin McCain (left)
David Richmond (right)

A section of the Greensboro lunch counter at the International Civil Rights Center & Museum

On the afternoon of February 1, 1960, the four students entered the Greensboro Woolworth's store. They walked around the department store and picked up items that they needed for their everyday use. They went to the cashier and made their purchases. Nothing they did caused any undue attention. Then they walked over to the lunch counter.

**FACT!**

Newspaper photographer Jack Moebes took the first photograph of the Greensboro protest. He caught the Greensboro Four leaving Woolworth's after the first day of the sit-in.

The white customers were quiet as the four young Black men approached the lunch counter. The Greensboro Four knew that all eyes were on them. McNeil, McCain, Richmond, and Blair moved forward. They calmly and politely took their seats, though they were terribly nervous inside. It may seem surprising today that such a harmless gesture was so dangerous. But at that time, remaining seated could get them arrested or even killed.

The young men politely ordered coffee. Not surprisingly, both the Black and white waitstaff directed them to the stand-up counter to take their order to go. But the men remained seated. The manager came over and tried to convince them to leave. But the men remained seated. By this point, the police had arrived, but they didn't arrest the young men. The Greensboro Four weren't technically breaking a law. The police didn't want to increase the tension of the situation. The men remained seated until the manager closed the store—early.

The sit-in continued after February 1st. On February 2nd, the protesters included (from left to right) Joseph McNeil, Franklin McCain, Billy Smith, and Clarence Henderson.

## "Disappointed"

At one point during the first day of the sit-it, an old white woman approached McCain at the lunch counter. He guessed she was going to say something insulting. In fact, she told the young men that she was disappointed in them. But when McCain asked her why, her response surprised him. She said, "I'm disappointed it took you so long to do this."

# Chapter 4
# A MOVEMENT IS BORN

The four young men had not expected the first day of their protest to go as well as it had. They had thought they would be arrested, beaten, or even killed. As the store closed, they felt proud of what they had done.

Sitting down that first day took a lot of courage. But the Greensboro Four knew that it was going to take more than one day of protesting to change things. They also knew they would need more people involved for the protest to make a real difference.

After talking to other students on campus, the four men returned to Woolworth's the next day to sit at the counter again. This time, the Greensboro Four had about 20 people with them.

Franklin McCain (front) and other protesters at the Greensboro Woolworth's lunch counter

By the fourth day of the protests, the lunch counter sit-in at the Greensboro Woolworth's had grown by leaps and bounds. More than 300 students from local schools had joined the protest. The schools included North Carolina A&T, Bennett College, and Dudley High School. Even some white students from the Woman's College of the University of North Carolina joined the sit-in. The students protested both inside and outside of the store.

Days passed, and the sit-in continued. Many white customers grew angry. Some were aggressive toward protesters. They would yell racial **slurs**, throw things, or pour drinks on them. But the protesters sat peacefully. They knew their power came from not reacting to insults or attacks. Some days, white people would show up early to take a seat at the counter before the protesters arrived. But the protesters kept coming back. The **Ku Klux Klan** even showed up to try to scare them. But the protesters just sat calmly.

The Greensboro protesters inspired others to do the same. Professor John R. Salter (seated on left) was sprayed with ketchup and mustard while protesting segregation at a lunch counter in Mississippi in May 1963.

A group of female students sitting in at the Greensboro Woolworth's lunch counter to protest segregation

Day after day, the protesters were refused service. But the peaceful movement grew. At one point, as many as 1,000 students showed up at the store to protest. They took turns sitting inside at the lunch counter. Others crowded around them. The sit-in took a huge toll on Woolworth's business. Many people avoided going downtown altogether to avoid the crowds.

**FACT!**
On February 1, 2020, the Google Doodle honored the famous protest with a miniature 3D exhibit of the Greensboro lunch counter sit-in. It featured art from artist Karen Collins, founder of the African American Miniature Museum.

As the protest continued, local and national news coverage of the event began to spread. All over the South, young people were hearing about the Greensboro sit-in. They were inspired to do similar protests.

Future activist Julian Bond was a student at Morehouse College in Atlanta, Georgia. He had read about the Greensboro Four in the newspaper during the first week of the protest. He joined a group of other students to begin similar sit-ins in Atlanta. In Nashville, Tennessee, future civil rights activists Diane Nash and John Lewis had their first sit-in on February 13.

Civil rights activist Julian Bond in 1966

Unfortunately, the protests did not always stay peaceful. On February 27, at a sit-in in Nashville, angry white customers beat a group of protesters. But when the police showed up, they didn't arrest the white people. They arrested the Black protesters for charges such as resisting arrest and disorderly conduct. This was John Lewis's first arrest.

Black protesters stage a sit-in at a whites-only lunch counter in Nashville, Tennessee.

**FACT!**

Representative John Lewis served in the U.S. House of Representatives for 33 years. He was arrested 40 times over the course of his career as a leader and civil rights activist.

The arrests didn't stop people from protesting. In fact, they had the opposite effect. People were angry that peaceful protesters would be arrested, while those who beat them remained free. By the end of the day on February 27, 1960, 98 protesters had been thrown in jail. But 500 more took their place in downtown Nashville.

Additional protest movements spread to 55 cities in 13 states in two months. Even in New York City, where segregation was already illegal, protesters showed up outside Woolworth's stores to support the movement. Across the country, young people were inspired to see how they could band together to make social change happen. And they didn't stop at lunch counters and restaurants. People protested segregation in hotels, beaches, libraries, and other businesses and public places.

All over the United States, protesters—mostly young people—were showing that it was time for a change. They were speaking out against racism to show that people of all colors deserved equal treatment and the same rights.

Protesters carry signs against segregation outside a Woolworth's store in New York City.

## Nashville Protests

The protests in Nashville continued throughout the spring of 1960, as they did in Greensboro. Many protesters were arrested. Tensions reached an all-time high when someone bombed the house of civil rights attorney Z. Alexander Looby.

Looby's house damaged by bombing

Thousands of angry protesters swarmed the city's courthouse. Diane Nash confronted Mayor Ben West. She asked him, "Do you feel that it's wrong to discriminate against a person, solely on the basis of his race or color?" The mayor admitted he did indeed think it was wrong. Three weeks later, lunch counters throughout Nashville were integrated.

# Chapter 5
# SPURRING CHANGE

Perhaps the Woolworth's owners were tired of all of the publicity. Perhaps it was because they had lost money during the protests. Or perhaps they realized that integrating the lunch counter was the right thing to do. It is unknown exactly why, but after months of public protests and national coverage, Woolworth's officially integrated the lunch counter in Greensboro, North Carolina.

Geneva Tisdale, a former cook at the Greensboro Woolworth's, toured the opening of the International Civil Rights Center & Museum in Greensboro in 2010.

A Student Nonviolent Coordinating Committee meeting

The change was made quietly in July 1960, as most of the protesting college students had gone home for the summer. The first Black people to be served at the counter were actually Woolworth's employees. They were Geneva Tisdale, Susie Morrison, Anetha Jones, and Charles Best.

Black people could now be served at the previously whites-only lunch counter. A year before, such a change would have seemed impossible. But the sit-ins showed what could be done when people used peaceful protests to fight for justice. Many of those protesters had been young people. The success of the Greensboro protest helped inspire students in Raleigh, North Carolina, to form the Student Nonviolent Coordinating Committee (SNCC).

The Greensboro protests ended segregation at many local businesses. But segregation still went on in many places throughout the South. Groups such as the SNCC, CORE, and the NAACP continued their nonviolent protests in order to challenge segregation everywhere.

By 1961, the U.S. Supreme Court had banned segregation in buses traveling between states. It had also banned it in bus station restaurants and bathrooms. But places in the South still illegally allowed segregation. Later that year, brave men and women, both Black and white, boarded buses and rode throughout the South. They were called Freedom Riders. They demanded service at restaurants. They challenged segregated and water fountains.

Freedom Riders gather outside their burning bus in Alabama.

What they were doing was dangerous. On May 14, 1961, angry white people bombed a bus carrying Freedom Riders. White mobs attacked them several other times. Police even arrested the riders. Eventually, the National Guard came to protect them.

Peaceful protests continued throughout the country. The biggest of all was the March on Washington. In August 1963, 250,000 people crowded in front of the Lincoln Memorial to protest the racial discrimination Black Americans still faced, especially regarding jobs.

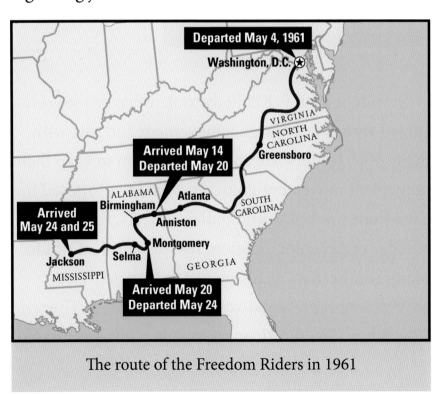

The route of the Freedom Riders in 1961

John F. Kennedy

President John F. Kennedy took office in 1961. He agreed with the civil rights movement and met with many of its leaders. He encouraged them to keep their nonviolent movement going. In 1963, he proposed the Civil Rights Act. It would outlaw any discrimination based on race, color, religion, sex, or nation of origin. Many Southerners were angered by this act. Their government representatives fought against it. Then, in November 1963, President Kennedy was **assassinated**.

President Johnson signed the Civil Rights Act of 1964.

President Lyndon B. Johnson took office and continued Kennedy's work on the Civil Rights Bill. Finally, in 1964, the years of protests, patience, strength, and determination paid off. The U.S. Congress passed the Civil Rights Act. This meant that all Americans had the legal right to equal access to jobs, schools, housing, and public places. It didn't end racism, but it did mean that Black Americans finally had the law on their side. The brave actions of four men at an ordinary lunch counter had sparked great change.

## FACT!
Five years after President Kennedy's death, Dr. Martin Luther King Jr. was also assassinated.

## Chapter 6
# HONORING AND PRESERVING HISTORY

The lunch counter at the Greensboro Woolworth's sat undisturbed for more than 30 years. It was a quiet symbol of a small protest that blossomed into a student-led civil rights movement. But in October 1993, the Woolworth's in Greensboro, North Carolina, went out of business.

The former Woolworth's building in Greensboro stood empty in 1994.

When the store shut its doors, it took a piece of civil rights history with it. Members of the Smithsonian Institution decided to meet with Black community leaders and City Council members in Greensboro.

After many talks, they all agreed that the lunch counter needed to be preserved for historic purposes. An 8-foot (2.4-meter) section of the lunch counter would be removed from the former Woolworth's store. Four stools would also be taken out to represent the Greensboro Four at the lunch counter sit-ins. The lunch counter and stools would be displayed at the Smithsonian in Washington, D.C.

But how would they remove a counter and stools, preserve them, and move them to a museum hundreds of miles away?

To transport these historic pieces, special crates had to be built. These crates would protect the lunch counter and stools from being damaged. Packing materials were used inside the crates to cushion and protect the pieces.

A museum **curator** took pictures of all the objects that would be moved to the Smithsonian. That way, each item in the crates could be properly identified.

Next, a crew took apart the lunch counter and stools and packed them in their crates. The curator labeled, numbered, and placed photographs on each crate to identify each piece.

From there, the crates were loaded into a truck and driven to the museum. Once the crates were unloaded, the section of the lunch counter and the stools where the Greensboro Four sat were put back together.

Today, this section of counter and stools are properly restored and maintained with cleaning and repairs to preserve their quality. They are displayed at the National Museum of American History in Washington, D.C.

The Greensboro lunch counter exhibit at the National Museum of American History

# Civil Rights Timeline 1948–1960

| 1948 | 1954 | 1955 | 1960 |
|---|---|---|---|
| President Truman's Executive Order 9981 ends segregation in the military. | Supreme Court case *Brown v. Board of Education* ends segregation in schools. | Rosa Parks spurs the Montgomery city bus boycott, ending segregation on city buses. | The Greensboro Four stage a sit-in at the local Woolworth's lunch counter, inspiring similar protests throughout the nation. |

Also in 1993, activists founded Sit-In Movement, Inc. They hoped to make something more of the old Woolworth's building. Over time, the organization had help from other contributors, including North Carolina A&T State University. Eventually, they made the building into a museum. The International Civil Rights Center & Museum officially opened on February 1, 2010—50 years after the Greensboro Four started the famous sit-in. The museum contains another section of the lunch counter and stools.

Civil rights activists, including Franklin McCain (far left) and Ezell Blair Jr. (now known as Jibreel Khazan, far right), cut the ribbon to open the International Civil Rights Center & Museum.

The museum has two goals. First, it wants to collect and preserve civil rights artifacts. It also wants to continue the fight for civil rights today. According to the executive director, Bamidele Demerson, the museum pictures a future free of discrimination and prejudice, where all people enjoy equal rights and freedom.

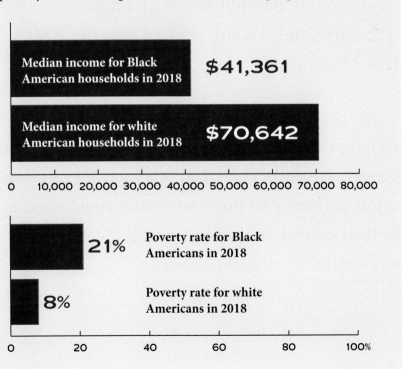

## The Struggle Continues

While civil rights have come a long way, Black Americans still struggle more than white Americans when it comes to jobs. In 2018, the average income for Black people was much lower and the poverty rate much higher than it was for white people.

Median income for Black American households in 2018 — $41,361

Median income for white American households in 2018 — $70,642

0   10,000  20,000  30,000  40,000  50,000  60,000  70,000  80,000

21% — Poverty rate for Black Americans in 2018

8% — Poverty rate for white Americans in 2018

0   20   40   60   80   100%

The Woolworth's building and the lunch counter it housed were the stage upon which the Greensboro Four acted. The men themselves are also remembered for history's sake. In 2002, the Greensboro Four were honored with a monument at North Carolina A&T State University.

Greensboro resident and artist James Barnhill created a 15-foot (4.6-m) tall bronze sculpture. It brings to life the photo that Jack Moebes took on the first day of the sit-in. The monument honors the Greensboro Four's courage and bravery in fighting for civil rights. Barnhill named his sculpture "February One." It is also referred to as the "A&T Four Monument."

Many people spoke at the unveiling of the sculpture, including the university's **provost**, Carolyn Meyers. She said, "Forty-two years ago, four freshmen at this university sat down so that we could stand up. By their chapter in history, a new day in civil rights was written."

James Barnhill's sculpture "February One"

## FACT!

In 2019, artist Nils Westergard painted a mural of Moebes's photo of the Greensboro Four sitting at the lunch counter. It is painted on the outside wall of the Windsor Recreation Center in Greensboro.

# Chapter 7
# THE GREENSBORO FOUR

The Greensboro Four made a big difference at a young age. But what did they go on to do after that?

In 1963, Joseph McNeil completed his degree in engineering physics from North Carolina A&T. He then joined the Air Force and moved to New York State. McNeil worked for the Federal Aviation Administration for 15 years. When he retired from the Air Force Reserves, he had earned the rank of major general. McNeil and his wife, Ina, have five children.

Joseph McNeil

Jibreel Khazan,
formerly Ezell Blair Jr.

Ezell Blair Jr. earned his degree in sociology from North Carolina A&T in 1963. Several years later, he moved to New Bedford, Massachusetts. There he joined the Islamic faith and changed his name to Jibreel Khazan. He has worked with developmentally disabled people as well as large companies to create job opportunities for all. He and his wife, Lorraine, have three children.

> **FACT!**
> Joseph McNeil's son Franklin David McNeil is named after Franklin McCain and David Richmond.

Franklin McCain earned two degrees from North Carolina A&T—in chemistry and biology. He graduated in 1964. He moved to Charlotte, North Carolina, where he worked for a chemical company for 35 years. McCain also stayed involved in education, serving on several college boards throughout his life. He and his wife, Bettye, had three sons. She died in 2013. Franklin died in 2014.

David Richmond was the only one of the Greensboro Four to spend most of his life in that city. He was uncomfortable with the fame that came from the sit-ins. He never did graduate from college. He worked in Franklin, North Carolina, for seven years, training workers for jobs in public service. But Richmond eventually moved back to Greensboro to care for his aging parents. It was there he died of lung cancer at the age of 49. He left behind two children.

The four brave Black men went their separate ways, physically, but they were forever connected through friendship and bravery. Their choice to fight for what was right as young men continues to inspire countless people today. Their courage turned a simple lunch counter and stools into an inspiring symbol of the fight for racial justice.

David Richmond (left), Franklin McCain (center), and Joseph McNeil admire an exhibit of four of the original Woolworth's stools at the Greensboro Historical Museum.

## Contributors to Society

In 2010, the Greensboro Four received the James Smithson Bicentennial Medal. The medal is given to those who have made major contributions to society. McNeil, McCain, and Blair (now Khazan) received medals. David Richmond Jr. accepted the medal for his late father.

Medal ceremony for the Greensboro Four

The James Smithson Bicentennial Medal

# EXPLORE MORE

The National Museum of American History

## National Museum of American History

The National Museum of American History in Washington, D.C., has a Greensboro lunch counter exhibit and many others. Civil rights is a theme that runs through many exhibits. This includes topics such as racial justice and the struggles for disability rights, women's rights, and LGBT rights.

# Civil Rights Center & Museum

The International
Civil Rights
Center & Museum
in Greensboro,
North Carolina,
is housed in the
old Woolworth's
building. Its
permanent exhibits

The Greensboro lunch counter at
the Civil Rights Center & Museum

focus on the Greensboro lunch counter and the civil
rights movement of the 1950s and 1960s. Temporary
exhibits have shined a light on homelessness and
shared Dr. Martin Luther King Jr.'s private papers.

# National Museum of African American History and Culture

For more information on Black American history
and contributions to American culture, check out
the National Museum of African American History
and Culture. This museum in Washington, D.C., holds
exhibits dedicated to African American influence in
politics, civil rights, music, culture, and more.

# GLOSSARY

**activist** (AK-tuh-vist)—a person who works for social change

**artifact** (AR-tuh-fakt)—a human-made object used in the past

**assassinate** (us-SASS-uh-nate)—to murder an important person

**curator** (KYER-aye-tuhr)—a person who helps with exhibits at museums and other places

**discrimination** (dis-kri-muh-NAY-shuhn)—treating people unfairly because of their race, country of birth, gender, disability, or sexuality

**integrate** (IN-tuh-grate)—to bring people of different races together in schools and other public places

**Ku Klux Klan** (KOO KLUX KLAN)—a group that promotes hate against African Americans, Catholics, Jews, immigrants, and others

**provost** (PRO-vost)—the person in charge of academics at a college or university

**racism** (RAY-siz-uhm)—the belief that one race is better than another race

**segregation** (seg-ruh-GAY-shuhn)—the practice of keeping groups of people apart, especially based on race

**slavery** (SLAY-vur-ee)—controlling people by denying them freedom and forcing them to work without pay

**slur** (SLER)—insulting name or word

**unconstitutional** (un-kon-stuh-TOO-shuhn-uhl)—a law that goes against something set forth in the Constitution

**vinyl** (VYE-nuhl)—a flexible, waterproof, shiny plastic that is used to make floor coverings, raincoats, and other products

# READ MORE

Krishnaswami, Uma. *Threads of Peace: How Mahatma Gandhi and Reverend King Changed the World.* New York: Atheneum Books for Young Readers, 2021.

Smith, Sherri L. *What Is the Civil Rights Movement?* New York: Penguin Workshop, 2020.

Smith-Llera, Danielle. *Lunch Counter Sit-ins: How Photographs Helped Foster Peaceful Civil Rights Protests.* North Mankato, MN: Compass Point Books, 2019.

# INTERNET SITES

*Commemorating the 50th Anniversary of the Woolworth Lunch Counter Student Sit-in*
youtube.com/watch?v=uH6Ur_Jq7dQ

*How Youth Activists Impacted the Civil Rights Movement*
biography.com/news/african-american-youth-civil-rights-movement

*Join the Greensboro Sit-ins*
youtube.com/watch?v=usVzJ3qngSU

# INDEX